Nimrod

From Enigma Variations

Arranged for Piano Solo

Edward Elgar

OPUS 36

NOVELLO PUBLISHING LIMITED
14–15 Berners Street, London W1T 3LJ, UK

Order No: NOV 100041 R

VARIATIONS

No. IX

(Nimrod)

Edward Elgar, Op. 36

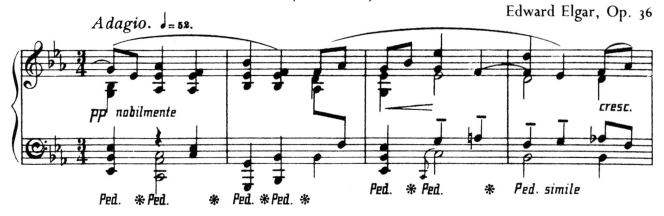

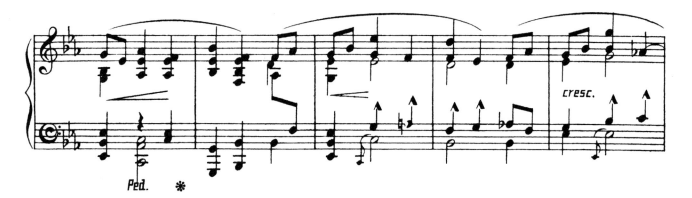

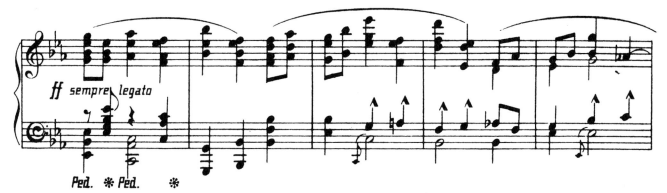

Edward Elgar (signature)

MUSIC FOR PIANO SOLO

ORIGINAL COMPOSITIONS

Allegro – Concert Solo
Music for Piano *an album of five pieces:*

> *My Song*
> *Carrisima*
> *Echo's Dream*
> *Rosemary*
> *Beau Brummel*

Presto and Griffinesque
Two piano pieces:

> In Smyrna
> Skizze

ARRANGEMENTS

Chanson de Matin *arranged by Thomson*
Chanson de Nuit *arranged by Thomson*
Enigma Variations, The *arranged by the composer*
Nimrod, *from The Enigma Variations, arranged by the composer*
Starlight Express, The *a suite for piano selected from the incidental music for the play. Arranged by Kettèlbey*
Elgar Piano Album *ten arrangements by Desmond Ratcliffe:*

Theme from Enigma Variations	Serenade from 'Wand of Youth' Suite 1
Nimrod	Angel's Farewell from 'The Dream of Gerontius'
Chanson de Matin	Canto Popolare from 'In the South'
Chanson de Nuit	Imperial March
Opening Theme from Symphony No 1	Adagio from the Cello Concerto